Good Question!

What Was America's Deadliest War?
AND OTHER QUESTIONS ABOUT . . .
The Civil War

STERLING CHILDREN'S BOOKS
New York

STERLING CHILDREN'S BOOKS
New York

An Imprint of Sterling Publishing
387 Park Avenue South
New York, NY 10016

Photo credits: The Granger Collection, New York: 16; iStockphoto.com © spxChrome: 22 background;
Library of Congress: 1, 12 top, 13 top and bottom, 21, 22, 30, 31, 32

ISBN 978-1-4027-9623-4 [hardcover]
ISBN 978-1-4027-9046-1 [paperback]

Distributed in Canada by Sterling Publishing
c/o Canadian Manda Group, 165 Dufferin Street
Toronto, Ontario, Canada M6K 3H6
Distributed in the United Kingdom by GMC Distribution Services
Castle Place, 166 High Street, Lewes, East Sussex, England BN7 1XU
Distributed in Australia by Capricorn Link (Australia) Pty. Ltd.
P.O. Box 704, Windsor, NSW 2756, Australia

Design by Elizabeth Phillips and Andrea Miller
Art by Robert Hunt

For information about custom editions, special sales, and premium and corporate purchases,
please contact Sterling Special Sales at 800-805-5489 or specialsales@sterlingpublishing.com.

Manufactured in China
Lot #:
2 4 6 8 10 9 7 5 3 1
10/13

www.sterlingpublishing.com/kids

CONTENTS

What was America's deadliest war?

The Civil War was the deadliest and most tragic war ever fought by Americans on U.S. soil. During a civil war, people from the same country go to battle against each other. The American Civil War was fought by two sections of the United States, one in the North and one in the South. It lasted less than five years (from 1861 to 1865), but more soldiers and sailors either died or were injured in this war than in all other combined wars fought by Americans.

By the mid-nineteenth century, the United States had grown into two very different regions. The North was made up of many lively towns and bustling port cities that attracted large populations. It was filled with factories and had dozens of railroads. The South had huge expanses of land and a climate that was good for farming. Its economy was based on enormous farms called plantations that grew crops such as cotton and tobacco. Many workers were needed to run these plantations. The South used millions of enslaved Africans to do the work.

Many people in the North saw slavery as morally wrong and were determined to end it. However, many Southerners believed they needed slavery to keep their way of life. They were determined to continue slavery. As a result, people in many Southern states were willing to break away and start their own country. More than anything else, it was this dispute over slavery that would lead to the Civil War.

A map of the nation shows how free and slave states were divided during the Civil War.

A NATION DIVIDED: 1861-1865

WASHINGTON TERRITORY

OR

CA

NV*

UTAH TERRITORY

COLORADO TERRITORY

DAKOTA TERRITORY

NEBRASKA TERRITORY

KS

NEW MEXICO TERRITORY

INDIAN TERRITORY

TX

MN

WI

IA

MO

AR

LA

MI

IL

IN

OH

KY

TN

MS

AL

GA

PA

NY

WV*

VA

NC

SC

FL

ME

VT

NH

MA

RI

CT

NJ

DE

MD

Washington, DC (Union capital)

Richmond (Confederate capital)

N
W · E
S

Free state that remained in the Union

Slave state that remained in the Union

Slave state that seceded from the Union

Territory not allowing slavery

Territory allowing slavery

West Virginia and Nevada were admitted into the Union during the Civil War.

Enslaved people picking cotton on a Southern plantation.

When did slavery begin in America?

The first enslaved people were brought to Virginia from Africa in August of 1619 to work on the earliest plantations. As America grew, so did the demand for workers. Since slavery was the cheapest form of labor, its use became widespread.

Most of the enslaved workers in America were captured in their native Africa and brought to America in chains. They were packed together below the deck on filthy, unsafe ships. The sea voyage lasted from two to three months. Hundreds of thousands died along the way. Those who survived were sold to the highest bidder. Often times, families were split up, separated forever.

These men, women, and children were forced to work without pay. On plantations, they planted and picked big-money crops, including cotton, tobacco, and sugar cane. All were forced into a life without freedom and many were violently mistreated by slaveholders.

When manufacturers learned to turn cotton into cloth, the whole world wanted it for clothing. As demand for cotton soared, the slaveholders needed more slaves to do the work.

What was the cotton gin and why was it important?

Even with the high demand for cotton, the Southern growers had a serious problem. Every boll (the fluffy part of the cotton plant) was full of seeds, which had to be removed by hand before the cotton could be used. It took many hours to do the job and a lot more slaves were needed for the work. It was difficult to make money growing cotton. Those who opposed slavery hoped that the plantation owners would stop growing cotton—and, in turn, free the slaves.

Then, in 1793, inventor Eli Whitney developed a machine called a cotton gin. The new device pulled all the cottonseeds from the bolls with great speed and made the cotton growers richer than ever. This meant more cotton plantations—and a desire for even more slaves.

Why did the South rebel?

By 1860, the North and the South had drawn further apart than ever before. One of the greatest issues was slavery, and the country had reached a turning point. It was an election year, and the new president of the United States would help determine the fate of slavery.

The Republican Party's candidate for president was Abraham Lincoln, a remarkable man who came from humble beginnings. He taught himself to be a lawyer and was a brilliant speaker. Lincoln was also a man of strong beliefs. He felt that the United States should stay together as one union. But he also believed that slavery was wrong and said, "As I would not be a slave, so I would not be a master." As a politician, Lincoln delivered powerful speeches against slavery that excited many people.

On November 6, 1860, Abraham Lincoln was elected president of the United States, which enraged the South. Many Southerners refused to accept a president who was against slavery. Between December 1860 and June 1861, eleven Southern states rebelled against the United States. They left the Union to form their own independent nation. These states, from first to last, included South Carolina, Mississippi, Florida, Alabama, Georgia, Louisiana, Texas, Virginia, Arkansas, North Carolina, and Tennessee. This act of separating themselves from the rest of the country was called secession. The new nation was called the Confederate States of America, and Jefferson Davis was made its president.

The unthinkable had happened. The United States of America had split in two: the Union states of the North and the Confederate states of the South. Their bitter disagreement over slavery pushed both sides toward civil war.

Abraham Lincoln taking the presidential oath of office at his inauguration.

Confederate troops fire upon Fort Sumter.

Who fired the first shots of the Civil War?

The first shots fired in the Civil War took place in South Carolina. The state had seceded from the Union, but Northern troops were still at Fort Sumter, a fortress in Charleston Harbor. South Carolina's Confederate governor demanded that the Union troops leave. But Union officials ordered them to stay and hold the fort.

On April 11, 1861, Brigadier General P.G.T. Beauregard demanded that the Union commander of the fort, Major Robert Anderson, surrender to the Confederate forces. But the major refused. The next day Confederate cannons placed around the harbor started bombarding Fort Sumter. They were the first shots fired between the Union and Confederacy. The Civil War had begun.

Did brother fight against brother in the war?

The Civil War not only divided the nation. It also divided thousands of families whose members held different views about slavery. Some bitterly opposed it. Others strongly supported it. Some went to war to support their views. Brothers fought against brothers. Cousins fought against cousins. And, sometimes, fathers even fought against sons. Family disagreement about the war reached all the way up to the White House. President Lincoln's wife, Mary Todd Lincoln, lost three of her brothers who died fighting for the Confederacy.

Some brothers served as generals on opposing sides. In many battles, brothers fought against each other. At the Battle of Fort Royal, Confederate General William Goldsborough captured a Union infantryman, who turned out to be his brother Charles. Confederate General John Morgan led a violent raid on a Union fort in Kentucky. Many Union soldiers were killed, including Morgan's brother, Thomas.

Who were the leaders of the war?

ABRAHAM LINCOLN
(1809–1865)

Lincoln was president of the United States during the Civil War. Despite many setbacks, he led the Union to victory and made the nation whole again. In the process, Lincoln freed millions of enslaved people. Just days before the official end of the war, Lincoln was assassinated. Today, he is regarded as one of the greatest American presidents.

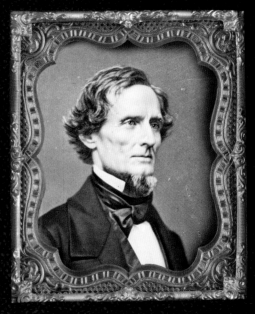

JEFFERSON DAVIS
(1808–1889)

Davis was president of the Confederate States of America during the Civil War. Before the war, he served as a U.S. Senator from Kentucky and was the secretary of war from 1853 to 1857. Davis was not an effective president because he did not work well with other members of the new Confederate government. But after the war, he did the nation a great service. He worked hard to convince the defeated South to become loyal to the Union.

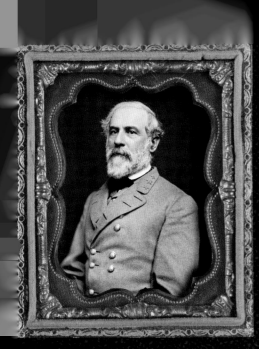

ROBERT E. LEE
(1807–1870)

e was commander of all the
onfederate forces during the Civil
Var. He was regarded as a superb
ry leader and both the North and
outh wanted him to command
troops. But as a loyal Virginian, he
e to lead the Confederate troops.
as the most skilled of all the Civil
generals—even though the South

ULYSSES S. GRANT
(1822–1885)

Grant was the most effective ge
the Union had. Lincoln made h
General-in-Chief in March 186
was largely responsible for the Un
winning its final victory. On April 9
Lee surrendered to General Grant
Appomattox Courthouse in Virginia
Four years after the war ended, Gr
elected president of the United Sta

What was the first major battle of the war?

The shelling of Fort Sumter marked the start of the war, but it was not a battle in which men fought face to face. The war's first real battle took place near Manassas Junction, Virginia, and is often called the First Battle of Bull Run.

When the war began, both the North and South felt certain its army would have a quick, easy victory over the other side. On the morning of July 21, 1861, Union commanders, hearing that a Confederate force was camped near Manassas Junction, ordered their troops to march out of Washington, D.C. When reporters, officials, and some local people heard that a battle was about to take place, they gathered on a hillside to watch what they thought would be the first, and possibly the last, battle to be fought in the war. They wanted to see history being made.

When the Union troops reached the camp, they started firing on the Confederate soldiers. A full-blown battle had begun. The shocked onlookers quickly scattered. The battle raged on all day, but neither side would give in. Then, late in the afternoon, more Confederate troops arrived. The exhausted Union soldiers were overwhelmed and fled for their lives all the way back to Washington, D.C.

Before the day was over, almost 850 soldiers had died and 4,000 were missing or wounded. A bitter lesson was learned that day. This would not be a quick and easy war. Worse yet, many more men would surely lose their lives.

Union and Confederate soldiers attack each other at the First Battle of Bull Run.

Union officers stand next to one of their deadly war cannons in Fair Oaks, Virginia.

How did new weapons and inventions change the war?

The Civil War was fought with the largest armies that had ever been assembled. In addition, newly developed technologies were used to fight the war. In fact, the Civil War has been called "the world's first modern war."

The Civil War was the first conflict in which the telegraph was used. In the past, troops had great difficulty staying in touch with each other. But with the telegraph, messages could be quickly sent from one battlefield to another. Commanders could now send orders to their troops no matter how far away they were.

The airplane had not been invented by the time of the Civil War. Instead, large air balloons were used to scout from the sky. Standing in a basket attached to a balloon, a soldier could silently soar high above enemy lines and report what the opposing side was doing.

The Civil War used newer and better types of artillery and arms. Improved cannons were bigger and could fire larger shells with greater accuracy. For the first time, soldiers using rapid-firing rifles could shoot bullets faster than ever before. The land mine, a device that exploded when soldiers stepped on it, was widely used for the first time during this war.

The greatest changes of all took place at sea. The Civil War was the first conflict in which a submarine sank an enemy ship. It was also the first time torpedoes were used to blow up ships from under the water. And it was the first time ironclad ships were used in battle. Unlike warships made of wood, the ironclads were covered entirely with metal so that cannonballs bounced off them. Some of these ironclads also had revolving metal-covered structures on top called turrets. Sitting inside a turret, sailors could stay protected while turning and firing their guns in all directions.

Where were the deadliest battles fought?

More than fifty major battles and some 500 smaller battles were fought during the Civil War. At the Battle of Antietam, fought on September 17, 1862 near Sharpsburg, Maryland, more than 23,000 Union and Confederate soldiers were either killed or wounded. It was the deadliest single-day battle, not just during the Civil War, but also in the nation's history.

The battle that produced the highest number of casualties over all was the Battle of Gettysburg. It was fought from July 1 to July 3, 1863, in and around Gettysburg, Pennsylvania. During the three-day battle, some 50,000 men were killed.

Sadly, dozens of other deadly battles were fought, which took thousands of lives on both sides. At the Battle of Chickamauga (September 19–20, 1863) more than 40,000 Union and Confederate soldiers were either killed or wounded. Nearly 32,000 men were killed or wounded at the Battle of Spotsylvania Court House (May 8–21, 1864).

During the Civil War many battles were fought at sea. The most important was the Battle of Hampton Roads, which was fought near the coast of Virginia from March 8 to March 9, 1862. It was the first battle ever between ironclad ships. The day before the battle began, the Confederate ironclad CSS *Virginia* had destroyed two huge Union wooden warships, killing some 240 Union sailors. The *Virginia* then left to search for other targets.

Suddenly, the Union navy's own ironclad appeared on the scene. It was called the USS *Monitor*. For the next two days, the two ironclads hammered away at each other, firing their heavy cannons. They even tried to ram each other. But the iron sides on each ship prevented any serious damage. Finally, both vessels withdrew.

Although the battle ended without either ship winning, naval warfare was changed forever. Soon all navies would abandon their wooden ships. The armored warships had arrived.

Ironclads clash in the Battle of Hampton Roads.

This young drummer boy fought for the Union.

Did young boys fight in the war?

A large number of Civil War soldiers from both sides were not men at all. They were boys, many less than fifteen years old. Although their enlistment was illegal, numerous lads, some as young as eight or nine, ran away from home to join the troops. Recruiting officers needing more soldiers often ignored a boy's young appearance and signed him up without checking his age.

The greatest number of boy soldiers became drummer boys. During a battle, they would beat out officers' commands on their drums. Certain drumbeats told the troops to charge. Others told them to fall back. Still others told them to remain in place. It was dangerous work, and many were wounded or killed in battle.

Some boys became real heroes. A twelve-year-old Union drummer boy named Johnny Clem was about to be captured at the Battle of Chickamauga. Suddenly he dropped his drum, grabbed a rifle, and shot his way to freedom. Newspapers throughout the North hailed him as "the brave drummer boy of Chickamauga."

Why were horses so important in the war?

During the Civil War, horses were almost as important as soldiers. They were essential for the fighting success on both sides. Horses transported guns and ammunition. They carried messages. Soldiers on horseback, called cavalry, were a key part of every battle.

Hundreds of thousands of horses were killed in the war. The soldier who lost the most number of horses was Confederate General Nathan Bedford Forrest. During the war, he had thirty horses shot out from under him.

Stories of horses owned by military leaders were popular topics. One involved Union General George Meade's horse, Baldy, who was seriously wounded five times. Yet he recovered each time and carried Meade into his next battle. Another legendary tale involves Confederate General J.E.B. Stuart's horse, Virginia. When Union soldiers surrounded the general and were about to capture him, Virginia suddenly leaped over an enormous ditch and carried Stuart to safety.

Baldy, General George Meade's horse, stands ready for action in 1863.

An 1888 print honors Lincoln's historic
Emancipation Proclamation of 1863.

How did Lincoln help to end slavery in America?

Abraham Lincoln hated the practice of slavery. As a young man, he traveled to the city of New Orleans, which was home to more than 200 slave dealers. While in the city, Lincoln was shocked to see long lines of enslaved people being sold like cattle to the highest bidder. He had never been so horrified and outraged, and he vowed to rid the country of slavery. "If I ever get a chance," he said, "I'm going to hit this thing. And I'm going to hit it hard."

As the year 1862 ended, Lincoln, now president, decided to carry out the vow he had made as a young man. On January 1, 1863, he signed the Emancipation Proclamation, which set millions of enslaved people free. It declared "all persons held as slaves within any State or designated part of a State . . . in rebellion against the United States, shall be . . . forever free." This meant only slaves living in Confederate states were declared free. But they had to wait until Northern forces defeated the areas where they were held.

Unfortunately, the reach of the Emancipation Proclamation was very narrow. It did not include the entire Union. The proclamation also did not address slavery in territories that were still waiting to enter the Union as new States.

Many in his own government thought Lincoln had acted too hastily. They thought he should have waited until the war was won. But Lincoln was secure in his decision.

The Emancipation Proclamation was not a perfect document, but it was a beginning. Soon, amendments to the U.S. Constitution were passed that supported Lincoln's proclamation. In 1865, the Thirteenth Amendment formally abolished all slavery in the United States. In 1868, the Fourteenth Amendment gave citizenship to the former slaves, granting them the same rights and privileges as all other Americans. Today, the Emancipation Proclamation is considered one of the great documents of human freedom.

Did black soldiers fight in the war?

After President Lincoln issued the Emancipation Proclamation, the Union began to recruit black soldiers and sailors. More than 180,000 formerly enslaved men joined the Union forces, and more than 40,000 of them died fighting for their freedom.

One group of black soldiers became famous for their bravery. They were all members of the 54th Massachusetts Infantry, a fighting unit led by a white officer named Colonel Robert Gould Shaw. He knew that many white people doubted if these black men would make good soldiers. Shaw wanted to prove them wrong. He believed his men of the 54th were equal to any other group.

These men had their first fight on July 16, 1863, at the Battle of James Island in South Carolina. They fought with great courage as they drove back a Confederate attack.

On July 18, 1863, they were ordered to lead an attack on Fort Wagner, an important Confederate stronghold on Morris Island, South Carolina. Before the attack began, Colonel Shaw addressed his men. "I want you to prove yourselves," he told them. "The eyes of thousands will look on what you do tonight."

During the battle that followed, many of the men of the 54th became heroes. One of them was former slave William Carney. When the man carrying the regiment's flag was killed, Carney quickly grabbed it and continued on. Even when he was shot in his arm, leg, and chest, Carney carried the banner throughout the entire battle. His proudest boast was that the flag never once touched the ground.

Before the Second Battle of Fort Wagner was over, more than 1,500 members of the 54th were killed. Among them was Colonel Shaw. But his men fulfilled his great wish. They had proven they could fight as well and as bravely as any soldier.

Members of the 54th Massachusetts black regiment rush at Confederate troops.

President Lincoln at
Gettysburg, Pennsylvania.

Why is Lincoln's Gettysburg Address such a powerful speech?

In July 1863, one of the war's fiercest battles was fought in Gettysburg, Pennsylvania. Two months later, Abraham Lincoln received a letter, telling him that a cemetery in Gettysburg was being established to honor those who had been killed there. He was invited to deliver "a few appropriate remarks" at the dedication.

The ceremony took place on November 19, 1863. Lincoln listened patiently to the first speaker, who spoke for more than two hours. Then it was Lincoln's turn to address the people. Little did he know the speech he was about to deliver would be remembered forever.

Lincoln began his speech by reminding the huge crowd that the United States was "conceived in Liberty." He stated that it was founded on the idea "that all men are created equal." He declared that the cemetery was being dedicated to "those who here gave their lives that that nation might live."

Lincoln then urged the nation to make sure "that these dead shall not have died in vain." He stated that Americans had to make certain "that this nation shall have a new birth of freedom . . ." He ended with words that have become among the most famous ever spoken. The most important task of all, he said, was to ensure "that government of the people, by the people, for the people, shall not perish from the earth."

When Lincoln finished speaking, he did not receive loud applause. He was sure the speech had been a failure. But he was very wrong. No one remembers a word the other man spoke that day. Yet Lincoln's speech, which was only ten sentences long and contained fewer than 300 words, is widely regarded today as one of the greatest speeches of all time.

Many soldiers died from disease as well as from battle wounds.

Why did so many people die in the war?

More than 350,000 Northerners and some 250,000 Southerners died in the Civil War. Tens of thousands lost their lives on the battlefields. But the greatest number by far actually died from disease or poor medical attention.

The Civil War was fought at a time when people, including doctors, still knew very little about how infections were spread. Doctors received less training than today, and most of the medical instruments used today had not yet been invented. Also, there were very few military doctors. The entire Union army had only 98 medical officers, while the Confederacy had only 24.

Doctors also knew almost nothing about what caused spreadable diseases. It's no surprise that disease became the greatest killer of the Civil War. During the conflict, twice as many men died from disease than from gunshot wounds.

The most common diseases were typhoid fever, small pox, tuberculosis, malaria, and dysentery. They were caused by the unclean conditions of the soldiers' camps. Another cause was the poor quality of the soldiers' food and water. Few people knew these things could cause and spread disease.

However, disease was not the only great killer. Hundreds of thousands of men died in surgery. Doctors did not understand how important cleanliness was when performing operations. They did not clean out wounds before operating on them. They did not clean their instruments. They did not even wash their hands. Germs were easily spread, which often led to death after a wounded soldier was treated.

Still, even with poor practices, surgeons were able to save some of their patients. But there were far too few doctors, and thousands of wounded men died before they could even reach surgery.

How did America's deadliest conflict end?

By the middle of 1864, it looked like the North would win the war because it had more men and more weapons than the South. Still, the Union could not attain that one final victory.

Then, in August 1864, Union general William Sherman led over 60,000 men to Atlanta, Georgia, capturing the vital Confederate city. Sherman's soldiers demolished everything in their path. Sherman's victory increased President Lincoln's popularity and, in November, the president was elected for a second term. Sherman continued his destructive march from Atlanta all the way to Savannah, Georgia, leaving much of the South in ruins.

In early April 1865, President Lincoln's top general Ulysses S. Grant and his army of 100,000 men marched to Richmond, Virginia and forced Robert E. Lee's exhausted army to flee the Confederate capital. On April 9, 1865, Robert E. Lee surrendered all the Confederate forces to Grant at Appomattox Courthouse. America's deadliest war was finally over.

But for the nation, there was little time to rejoice. Only six days after Lee's surrender, Abraham Lincoln was shot and killed while watching a play. His assassin was a well-known actor and Confederate supporter named John Wilkes Booth.

Unfortunately, Lincoln's death came at a time when the enormous task of bringing the Confederate states back into the Union still lay ahead. President Andrew Johnson, Lincoln's successor, tried to help rebuild the South as quickly as possible. But many government leaders who supported the Union wanted to punish the South and make it difficult for the once Confederate states to return to the Union. But, to their credit, these government leaders also wanted to safeguard freedom for formerly enslaved people.

After a period of rebuilding called the Reconstruction Era, the Confederate states became part of the Union. And when the Fifteenth Amendment was passed in 1870, African American men gained the right to vote. Lincoln's hope for a free and united nation had been achieved.

CIVIL WAR TIMELINE

1619   AUGUST   ⋮   The first enslaved Africans are brought to Virginia.

1793   JUNE 20   ⋮   Eli Whitney applies for a patent for his cotton gin.

1860   NOVEMBER 6   ⋮   Abraham Lincoln is elected president of the United States.
      DECEMBER 20   ⋮   South Carolina secedes from the Union. Ten other Southern states will follow.

1861   FEBRUARY 4   ⋮   The Confederate States of America is formed.
      APRIL 12   ⋮   Confederate forces fire on Fort Sumter. The Civil War begins.
      APRIL 22   ⋮   Robert E. Lee becomes commander of the Confederate forces.
      JULY 21   ⋮   First Battle of Bull Run (Manassas Junction) takes place.
      NOVEMBER 6   ⋮   Jefferson Davis is elected president of the Confederate States of America.

1862   MARCH 8-9   ⋮   Battle of Hampton Roads takes place.
      SEPTEMBER 17   ⋮   Battle of Antietam takes place.

1863   JANUARY 1   ⋮   Abraham Lincoln signs the Emancipation Proclamation.
      JULY 1-3   ⋮   Battle of Gettysburg takes place.
      JULY 18   ⋮   Massachusetts 54th Infantry attacks Fort Wagner.
      NOVEMBER 19   ⋮   Abraham Lincoln delivers his Gettysburg Address.

1864   MARCH   ⋮   Ulysses S. Grant is named commander of all Union armies.
      SEPTEMBER 2   ⋮   Union army captures Atlanta.
      NOVEMBER 8   ⋮   Abraham Lincoln is re-elected president of the United States.

1865   APRIL 3   ⋮   Union army captures Richmond.
      APRIL 9   ⋮   Robert E. Lee surrenders the Confederate forces to Ulysses S. Grant.
      APRIL 14   ⋮   Abraham Lincoln is shot by an assassin and dies the next day.
      DECEMBER 6   ⋮   Congress ratifies the 13th Amendment abolishing slavery.

For bibliography and further reading visit: www.sterlingpublishing.com/kids/good-question